THIS COLORING BOOK BELONGS TO

Dd

dog sledding

ear muffs

F f

fireplace

ice fishing

leg warmers

mittens

polar bear

reindeer

sledding

thermometer

undershirt

vest

winter

fox

yarn

zero degrees

let it snow

Made in the USA
Las Vegas, NV
08 January 2025